The Great Animal Rescue: **Operation Noah**

By Amai Palmer

The Great Animal Rescue: Operation Noah
© Amai Palmer 2023

God blessed them and said to them, "Be fruitful and increase in number; fill the earth and subdue it. Rule over the fish in the sea and the birds in the sky and over every living creature that moves on the ground."²⁹ Then God said, "I give you every seed-bearing plant on the face of the whole earth and every tree that has fruit with seed in it. They will be yours for food. ³⁰ And to all the beasts of the earth and all the birds in the sky and all the creatures that move along the ground—everything that has the breath of life in it—I give every green plant for food." And it was so. .

Genesis 1:28

Disclaimer

This narrative is based on events that happened in Africa. It involves, on one occasion, the death of an animal and, on another, an account of a human being gored by an animal. It is not my intention that it should distress or alarm the reader. It is, however, an honest and realistic account, written out of a genuine desire to share with future generations how important it is to appreciate the importance of saving animals when we can.

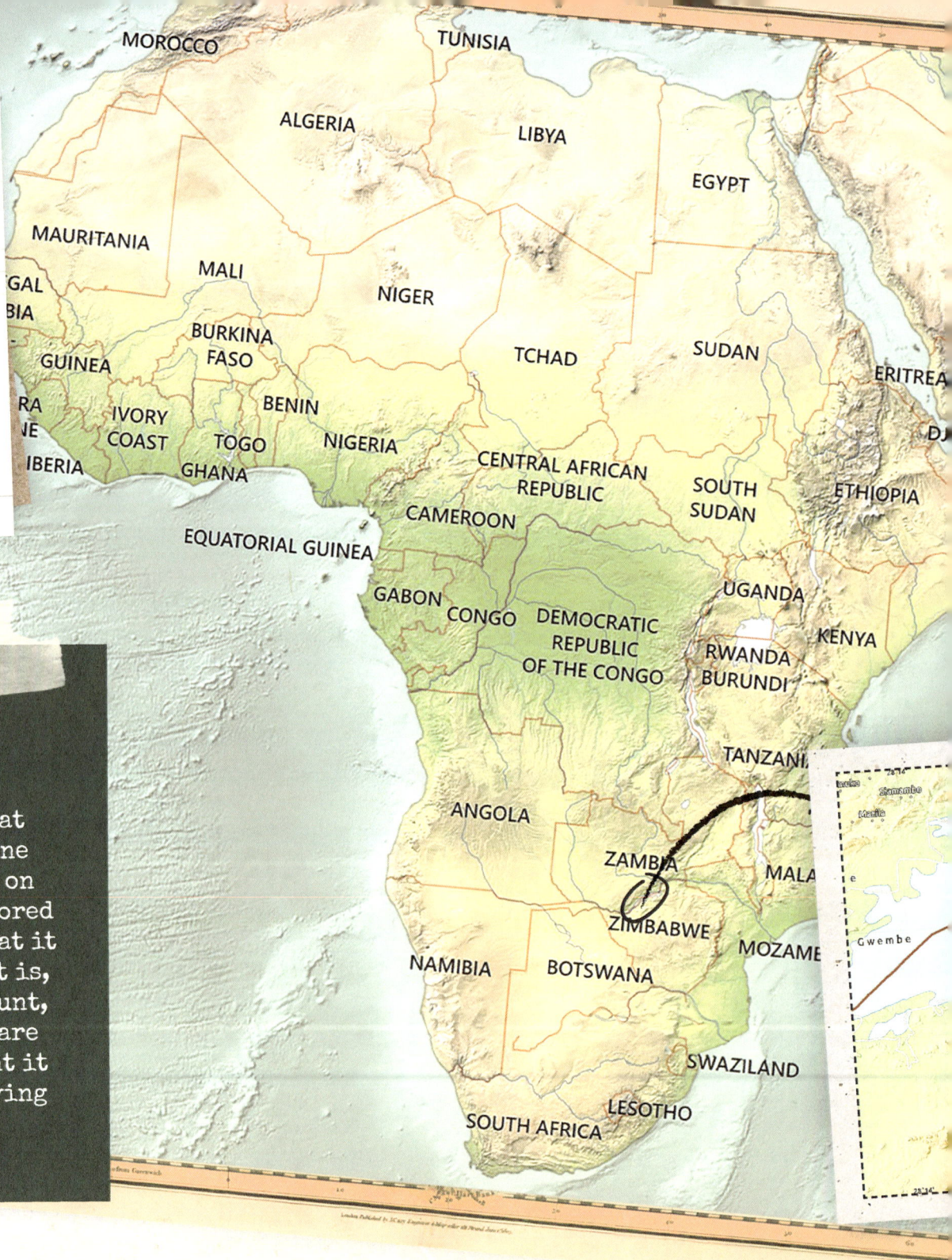

Table of Contents

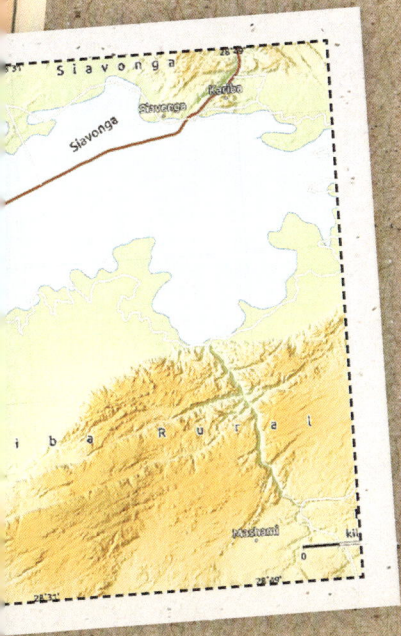

OPERATION AT KARIBA UN SUNDAY

LIFE

A HUGE AFRICAN WILDLIFE RESCUE: GALLANT MEN IN NOAH'S JOB

June 29, 1959

What was happening along the Zambezi River in Southern Rhodesia last week could be matched only by going back in biblical antiquity, to the time when" the waters prevailed exceedingly upon the earth" and Noah was herding all the animals into his ark. This time the flood was the work of man, and the Noahs were self-appointed - game rangers trying to rescue thousands of wild animals doomed to drown in a dammed-up lake. In the hot swampy country, thickly populated by all manner of beasts from aardvarks to warthogs, the rescuers toiled, forgetting the comfort, and often risking their lives in their huge humane task.

And THESE are the men who took over from NOAH

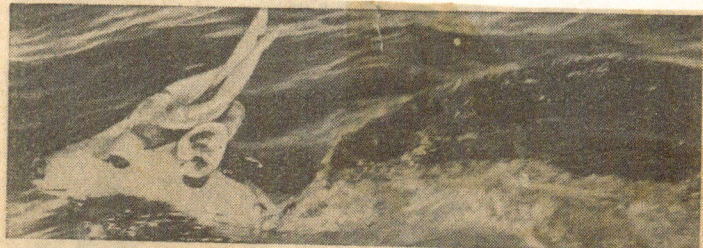

Continued from Page 4

python, fortunately non-poisonous, got him in the finger; another time, while swimming, a hissing sandsnake bit his lip.

This snake has deadly fangs; it waits until it has a good grip before ejaculating its venom.

Frank grabbed the snake's jaws and wrenched them open in time, suffering nothing worse than a punctured and swollen lower lip.

Rupert Fothergill showed similar presence of mind when one snake buried its fangs in his wrist. He prised his arm free, receiving nasty lacerations but avoiding much worse consequences.

Snakes were everyday headaches on Kariba. Once the boat was chugging peacefully along in midstream when a cry of sheer terror came from one of the Africans. Two striped sandsnakes had escaped from a sack in the stern and were hissing and slithering over the deck.

Pandemonium at once broke loose. Men and animals tumbled over each other in the melee. They even broke the boat's windscreen before Fothergill and Junor, taking one snake each, recaptured them.

Deadly

BY contrast, Frank— the man allergic to serum—was masterly in controlling his fear of these man-killing reptiles. During one drive he was sitting on a rock counting the heads of game that broke cover when he happened to glance down. A spitting cobra was gliding silently between his feet.

The deadly head and at least three feet of its sinuous body had already emerged. Frank had only to give one tiny start of surprise to be sprayed with venom. But he stayed absolutely still. And the snake moved through his legs and slithered off into the bushes without touching him.

In camp there were many such snake encounters. When Bredenkamp was with the rangers, he called to Frank one evening: "Hey, do you want a snake?" Frank Junor was established as the rangers' chief snake collector.

It was a Cape wolfsnake. Bredenkamp had discovered it in an ammunition box. Frank soon took charge, grabbing it

behind the head and throwing it into a sack.

Fothergill watched this, then went to change. In his boots under his camp-bed he found a puff-adder. A few minutes later, he caught a whipsnake in some rocks. Nothing unusual.

The black mamba, Africa's deadliest snake, abounds in the Kariba Valley.

If a mamba decided to treat a boat as a Noah's Ark and drop among the crew from its leafy sanctuary, the men had a split-second decision to make: whether to try to kill it or to jump overboard into waters where crocodile might be lurking.

Capturing a mamba—which moves with lightning rapidity— in a small, crowded boat calls for the maximum concentration because, once a mamba has struck, serum must be administered within a matter of

minutes if the victim's life is to be saved.

Other perils awaited the band once they set foot on shore. Clad only in shorts or swimming trunks, they were called upon to liberate a host of terrified animals apt to repay their ministrations with horn and tooth and claw.

The technique of dealing with the various species had to be learnt by trial and error; the penalty of error was painful, and possibly fatal.

The patrols that flushed the first islands to form on the lake found them abounding in game. Bushbuck, grysbok, warthogs, baboons, and monkeys started up in all directions as the African beaters advanced in line, shouting and banging drums and tins.

The landing party would drive the startled creatures into the lake, where rangers and scouts from the boats were waiting to dive overboard and swim after the refugees, steering them to the mainland.

Danger

THE shy bushbuck were

Frank Junor. He was the professional zoologist who surprised the buffalo who was not prepared to listen to explanations.

Rupert Fothergill. He was the professional game ranger, granite-hard and experienced in the ways of the wild.

The African scouts were invaluable. California — though perhaps without knowing it, saved the life of Frank Junor when the buffalo charged.

THESE THREE RISKED THEIR LIVES

buck by its horns or ears and hold it until one of his colleagues could get a firm grip on its hind legs.

Then the animal would be pulled over the side and a third helper would bind the front and hind legs together.

Rupert Fothergill's first moment of triumph occurred when, after a tough swim, he caught his first ant-bear. The battle in the water was a life-and-death struggle.

The ranger forced himself backwards through the water, keeping a grip on the end of his lariat. Gradually, he managed to tow the kicking, struggling, clawing beast into the shallows where a team of Africans was waiting to pounce on it.

The ranger had only his native wits and swimming prowess; his adversary could rely

on a ferocious bite and claws that could rip a man's stomach wide open.

Fothergill managed to cast a noose over the ant-bear's head and draw it tight. Immediately the beast—a huge 200lb. male— turned on its back and tried to claw him.

The ranger forced himself backwards through the water, keeping a grip on the end of his lariat. Gradually, he managed to tow the kicking, struggling, clawing beast into the shallows where a team of Africans was waiting to pounce on it.

This did not happen.

There were, however, many stark tragedies. Few baby monkeys and young baboons survived. They were not eaten by

Most of the creatures to become the first entries in the bulky ledger of mercy captures were bushbuck, genet cats, monitor lizards, monkeys, and the species that normally inhabit forest near a river.

But snakes were everywhere, and the inhabitants of Kariba township on a hill overlooking the dam site were terrified that their homes would be invaded.

other animals, as one visitor thought, but lost in the water due to their lack of strength.

Baboons employed "suicide squads" to kill and eat mambas and other snakes from which they would normally lope away in terror.

Short-sighted snakes, unable to see safer ground across the water, swam in desperate circles until they sank.

One major scientific discovery was soon apparent: all animals can swim, if only for a short distance, when their lives depend on it.

Champions are leopards, waterbuck, and bushbuck. These can cover up to 1½ miles. Elephant and kudu are also long-distance swimmers.

2-yard miss

MOST of the big "cats" are excellent swimmers, and quit the islands before the rangers' drives took place.

Fothergill and company were one day caught napping while flushing waterbuck. Rupert heard snarls from a patch of dense thornbush. Suddenly a yellow streak flashed before his eyes.

A leopard had catapulted out of the bush only two yards from him. Rupert's shout of warning had no effect on the line of African beaters. They were transfixed to the spot.

But, as the angry beast glared and bared its teeth at them— darting down the line and trying to break through the cordon —they scattered.

The leopard that preferred dry land leaped through a gap in the ranks and vanished.

After that, the presence of fresh "cat" spoor was regarded with considerable respect, as much respect as the far more familiar encounter with poisonous snakes.

The most fantastic of these

The shy Bushbuck were a special problem. They slid noiselessly into the water and lay silent till their rescuers had passed. But once "flushed," the rescue drill was the same—one of the Musketeers swam with the beast, then, when near the boat, held it by the tail while the others pulled it aboard.

occurred while a Bulawayo ornithologist, Mike Stuart-Irwin, was in the boat.

Rupert Fothergill was in the water, wrestling with a great dog baboon, and Frank Junor was swimming to his aid.

Brian Hughes, standing at the rudder of the boat, gave a sharp yell:

"Look out, a mamba...."

Hughes had spotted an 8ft. black mamba, one of the most deadly and speedy of snakes, streaking across the water surface towards them. The ornithologist had a rifle, and as Brian shouted, he saw the snake. The rifle whipped to his shoulder. Then Junor—in a scandalised voice — hollers back: "No, Mike, no. Leave it alone!"

The mamba was then only 20 yards from the two swimmers, heading straight in their direction—but Frank Junor was such a lover of snakes that he still did not want to "waste" such a fine specimen.

As the man with the rifle hesitated, Brian Hughes screamed again: "Shoot it, man, shoot it!" Stuart-Irwin took aim, pulled the trigger. The mamba twitched, lashed the water, then floated lifeless on the surface.

And Junor, having swum across, lifted the snake's carcass sadly: "What a pity!" he said: "an absolute beauty!"

Condensed from "Animal Dunkirk," by Eric Robins and Ronald Legge. (Herbert Jenkins, 21s.)

© 1959 Eric Robins and Ronald Legge.

NEXT WEEK

The charge of the frightened elephants.

Chapter One

The Ancient Path

Mai Guru, the oldest matriarch, had led her herd for many years along the ancient path. She knew, like her ancestors before, how important it was for the herd to keep moving because elephants eat about 150 kilograms of grass and leaves each day. They followed the ancient route that had been etched like Google Maps, into their minds. Mysteriously, it is passed down from generation to generation.

Mai Guru explained to her new calf, Shingi, as they plodded along, that they needed to keep moving so the plants that they had eaten from would have time to regrow. She encouraged them along with her deep rumblings. They could be heard and felt by other elephants several kilometres away.

The elephant herd came from the north and began to descend the steep mountain pass of the great Zambezi Valley in Africa. Mai Guru's oldest son looked forward to the Mufuti pods, his favourite treat. She knew that they could depend on these trees as they grew alongside the banks of the mighty Zambezi River, which never ran dry. The symphony of sounds as the water flowed by, and the smell of damp earth, put the herd in a good mood. Mai Guru's sister enjoyed wallowing in the mud to soothe her parched skin. The swim across the river would cool them, giving relief from the stifling heat of the valley.

What a shock it was to Mai Guru, as she approached the water's edge. Where there once was a steady

Watsei pods

SHINGI

MAI GURU

THE GREAT ZAMBEZI VALLEY

river bound within its banks, there was now a vast sheet of water! There were islands where there used to be hilltops, and bushes where there used to be groves of trees! She looked for a way around but could not find one. She chewed on some leaves from the tree next to her thinking about what to do.

Eventually, she decided she had no option but to lead her herd through the waters and trust that when they reached the other side, they would find the ancient path. She decided they would swim from island to island.

She waded into the shallow water signalling to the herd to follow. Despite her enormous weight, she did not become stuck in the mud because elephants have unique feet. As each foot takes the weight it bulges to spread the load, and when they lift the leg, it contracts again to release the suction.

Mai Guru encouraged Shingi to follow her. The water became deeper and deeper until the only part of her that remained above the surface was her trunk. An elephant's trunk is very versatile, and Shingi could use it as a hand or arm, and she could breathe through it. Now, she held it up like a snorkel, sucking in air, as she swam along. Sometimes, the water became shallow, and she could walk a little way, but then she would sink back down and need to swim with all her strength. She soon became very tired, and after a while, she rested her head on her mother's back.

A few times they got caught up in the branches of the trees that were underwater. Yet, they swam on and on, determined to reach land. Shingi became frightened; she was exhausted, and the tip of her trunk became pale.

This is what the LORD says: "Stand at the crossroads and look; ask for the ancient paths, ask where the good way is, and walk in it, and you will find rest for your souls.

Jeremiah 6:16 (NIV.)

Then, they heard a strange, unnatural sound. Boats appeared with game rangers on board. The boats frightened the elephants. Man was not to be trusted! But there was no way of escape. Mai Guru felt terror overtake her. She feared for her herd. She swam on with extra vigour trying to get away. The boats came from both sides, travelling slowly. They had no place to go except to swim through the gap left by the boats. A man in long trousers called to the other men to keep count.

Mai Guru – Grandmother; Shingi – Brave One

Chapter Two
Ready or Not

Between 1955 and 1959, a large concrete arch dam wall was constructed in the Kariba gorge on the Zambezi River to provide hydroelectricity to the bordering countries of Zambia and Rhodesia (now called Zimbabwe). Behind the dam wall, the waters of the Zambezi River rose, and the surrounding land began to flood. Animals fled to newly formed islands, but the water continued to rise, and these islands also disappeared below the surface.

Thus began the greatest animal rescue the world has ever seen. It was called Operation Noah. From 1958 to 1964, over 6000 animals (elephants, antelopes, rhinos, lions, leopards, zebras, warthogs, birds and snakes) were rescued.

In late 1958, a young scientist, Frank Junor, received an invitation to join Operation Noah. These are his recollections…

I received a telegram:

ATTN: FRANK JUNOR

YOUR SCIENTIFIC RESEARCH SKILLS ARE NEEDED
– STOP – PLEASE JOIN THE ANIMAL RESCUE TEAM –
OPERATION NOAH – STOP – MEET IN KARIBA – STOP

– ARCHIE FRASER.

Taking care of wildlife had always been a deep interest of mine. I accepted the challenge and joined the wildlife ranger team led by Rupert Fothergill. Arriving in Kariba, I saw immediately the huge floating mats of maize stalks, sticks, and grass sailing down the swollen Zambezi River. The air was filled with the smell of dead fish.

When the wildlife rangers and I went out on the Zambezi River, which was fast becoming Lake Kariba, we noticed a strange phenomenon.

In some spots, the water welled up like a fountain. I looked more closely and saw in many places that there was gas bubbling up from the lake bed. Upon investigation, I learned that the gas was helium which is normally trapped in the ground.

We watched to see how the animals would react to the rising waters. We found baboons and vervet monkeys clinging to trees along with snakes and leguaans. Leguaans are large grey lizards which constantly flick their tongues to taste the air to pick up scents. The work had begun! We had to save them, ready or not! The first animal scooped up out of the rising waters was a tiny duiker. They are delicate antelope, with soft grey fur, and spikey little horns. But boy can they kick!

KARIBA DAM

A family of Kudu being guided to safety.

On the 9th of December, we set out to see what animals we could find. We had very little equipment or experience in capture. The team plucked a variety of small animals out of the water. They lashed back with tooth and claw. We learned how to handle them through trial and error which sometimes left scratch marks on our arms and legs.

On arriving at the nearest island, we forged our way through partly submerged trees having no idea what we would find. The plan was one group of men would walk down the island beating tins and driving the animals into the water, and the other half of the team would wait to dive in after the escapees.

A man in the boat would be handed a writhing animal. As with many of the other smaller animals, he intended to grab it by the back of the neck, and then, drop it into a sack to be let go in a safe place away from the raging river. It wasn't easy. We soon found that the most effective way to capture monkeys and wild cats, like genet and serval cats, would be to grasp them by the tail. If they turned around to attack, the men would bob them under the water, just momentarily, to stop their panicked reactions at having been captured by a man.

Once we gained confidence, we began to rescue the bigger antelope out of the water. It took a team of at least three men. One held onto the horns or ears while another

Rescuing a porcupine

Rupert saving a Mopani Squirrel

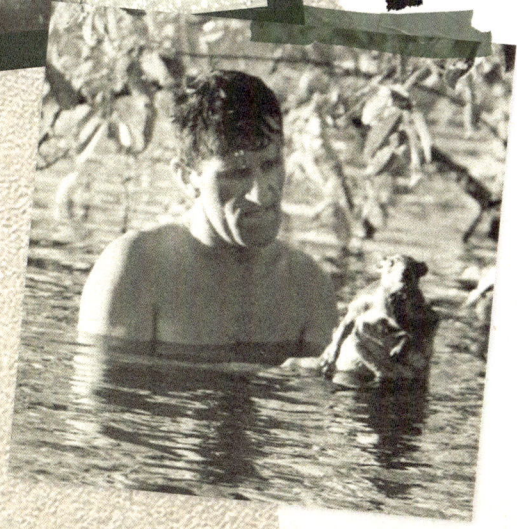

grabbed the hind legs. At the count of three, the animal would be hauled into the boat where a third man would bind the front and back legs together to stop them from harming themselves and the men. We needed to be very alert because the antelope would thrash about with very sharp hooves.

The task was enormous, and the team was overwhelmed by the possibility of the looming disaster if we failed to come up with more effective methods.

Diary entry – 12th December 1958

His Excellency, the Governor General, Lord Dalhousie, arrived at Kariba by Dakota. The plane was placed at the disposal of Ranger Bredenkamp, Fothergill, and myself. A flight over the course of the Sanyati river, the Matusadona range up the Sengwa river, and returning along the course of the Zambezi to Kariba, gave some indication of the size of the area to be covered during Operation Noah.

15

Chapter Three

Improving Capture

▲▽▲▽▲▽▲▽▲▽▲▽▲▽▲▽▲▽▲▽▲▽▲▽▲▽▲▽▲▽▲▽▲▽▲▽▲▽

On the 12th of January 1959, Rupert gathered the team around the campfire. "If we don't find a better way of rescuing larger numbers of animals at one time, thousands of animals will die. We need to 'make a plan'. So, after some discussion, we decided to use nets.

Early the next morning, we boarded the boats. The lake was calm, the reflections in the water were as clear as a mirror. Only the water lapping against the boat broke the tranquil silence. The day promised to be hot and sweaty. We cruised toward an island and glimpsed animals through the bush. The boats were jolted about by semi-submerged trees. There was double danger. We needed to avoid being thrown overboard if the boat hit a tree, and we had to keep watch as we passed under the branches, for snakes.

The plan was for one boatload of people to set up nets in the north of the island. We strung them between the trees and camouflaged them with branches and grass. The other boatload disembarked in the south. They took fuel cans and anything else that they could beat, making as much noise as possible. The plan was to 'flush out' the animals.

We lay in ambush. We had no idea what would come at us and whether the nets would hold. We had to pick our spots carefully to avoid the biting red ants. When the first clangs were heard in the distance, we readied ourselves to leap out from our hiding places. The sounds grew louder. Suddenly, they were joined by the snapping of bushes and the thundering of hooves.

CARRYING AN IMPALA TO THE BOAT

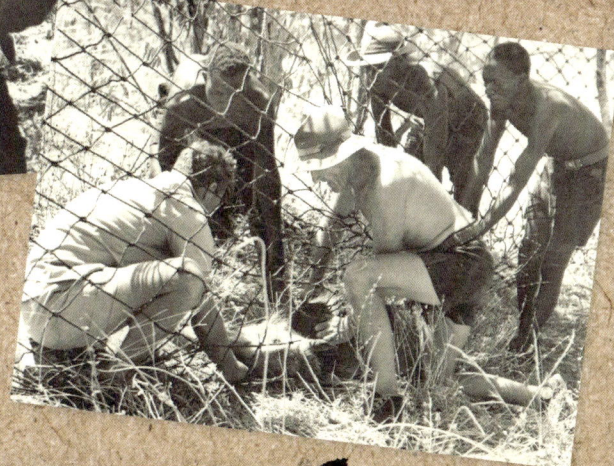

The first to spring into the nets were the graceful impala antelope, their white tails flashing as they hit the nets mid-leap. We sprang from our hiding places and pulled the nets over them. Some men held the animals to the ground while others quickly tied their front and back legs together using the stocking ropes. Once the animals' legs were secured in a way that would prevent them from harming themselves, each one was lifted onto the shoulders of a man. He ensured that he kept the animal's head up so it could breathe properly.

THE NETS

The warthogs, although smaller pig-like animals, were not as easy to capture as they put up a ferocious fight, kicking wildly and swinging their head from side to side wielding their razor-sharp tusks.

After they were weighed and tagged, I recorded all the information in carefully kept logbooks. It was tedious, but it provided information to future wildlife experts.

The animals were loaded onto the boats which sat dangerously low in the water. The longer an animal was tied up, the greater the risk of death. We had to move fast to minimise the shock the animals suffered.

The boats chugged towards the mainland. When we reached the shore, the animals were carried onto the land and the stocking ropes untied. Unfortunately, many of them were so disoriented that they ran back into the water.

"No!" we cried out in exasperation. We hadn't come this far only to have the animals drown. Rupert called to the boats to reverse and shepherd the animals back to shore.

LOADING ANIMALS ONTO A BOAT

Diary entry – 21st November 1958

I sat on a rock during one drive and tried to count the number of animals that broke cover. On looking down at one stage, a spitting cobra was passing through between my feet, so I sat still and let it slither under the rock on which I was perched.

Chapter Four

Methods Used in Capture

Dassies (Rock Hyrax):

Grasp by hind legs while swimming. Lift and keep holding the animal up. Duck, if it tries to bite, pop it into a sack.

Porcupines:

They need to be forced into the water, then a hand placed under the belly for support. The hind legs are grasped, and an open sack is pulled gently over the porcupine's head. The mouth of the sack is lifted along with the hind legs, and then, the whole animal slides into the sack. Porcupines need to be moved quickly into wooden or metal crates because they eat through sacks.

Mongooses:

Caught in a small scoop net, we must be fast as the animal jumps out quickly. When swimming after these animals they can easily be caught by the tail, and lifted, they can be shaken every time they attempt to bite. Also, wrap it in a sack and pop it in a box.

Baboons and monkeys:

While swimming on the surface the tail always sticks out above the water, so this is what we grasp to then pull the animal close to the boat, invariably, these animals try to grasp the boat with their hands and try to escape back into the water in all of the confusion. The head is therefore held down with the nose almost at water level—if the animal tries to turn we have to duck it and grab it behind the head by the scruff of the neck, then quickly let go of the tail and grasp behind the ears with two hands. Held firmly behind each ear, a large baboon is helpless. Push the animal into a sack, head first, then quickly close the mouth of the bag. During the process of placing a baboon in a bag, it is best if a helper grasps the two hands of the animal, and a second helper holds the bag open so that the baboon can be dropped into it suddenly.

Monkey

Baboon

For the creation waits in eager expectation for the children of God to be revealed.

Romans 8:19 (NIV)

Snakes:

Most snakes can be caught by the tail, but this is a dangerous practice as large specimens cannot always be lifted quickly into a confined space. For example, a boat that does not allow you to swing the reptile away from you if it attempts to bite.

Psammophis:

These are snakes, and they are liable to lose their tails if caught by them. These snakes seem to have a breaking joint, as in lizards. I have often forgotten this and been left with only a tail in my hand when trying to catch them. A few have been caught with healed stumps.

Hares:

Scoop net or grab by the ears and hold hind legs, as they can kick quite hard and have sharp nails on their hind feet. Langton catches them by the legs, when swimming, and holds all four legs, at once, in one hand. He seems to manage quite well.

22

Leguaans (monitor lizards):

Grab behind the head, and then, behind the shoulder. Place a finger under each leg. Easily caught by the tail and popped into a sack or box. Do not grab other lizards by the tail as that part of the body usually comes off (and grows back easily).

Antelope:

(Up to the size of adult Bushbuck rams)

In the boat, grab the hind leg then the other, lift so the head is above water, then grasp the front legs and tie up.

23

An impala in shock

Chapter Five

An Elephant's Observations

This new, vast, expanse of water has not been all bad for the elephant family. Huge stretches of open grazing grow on the shore, along with great carpets of water weed.

One glorious day, the herd was enjoying the sunshine and cooling off in the water whenever they became too hot. They were feasting and enjoying the peaceful atmosphere while the little ones frolicked in the mud. They squirted each other with showers of water sucked up with their trunks. From time to time, they were serenaded by the haunting cry of the Fish Eagle. Then, came the slightest sound, and as it grew louder, there was something familiar about it.

On the horizon emerged a series of black specks. As they drew closer, Mai Guru realised that it was a large boat towing five little boats. It looked like a mother duck with her ducklings. Were these the boats that guided them to safety? As the vessels drew close to the shoreline they stopped in the shallows. Men climbed out carrying large burdens.

Mai Guru observed more closely. She worked out they were animals bound by their legs. There were antelope such as impala, kudu, duiker and sable, along with warthog and aardvark (also known as ant bear). The men lowered them

gently into the shallow water and untied their restraints. They would thrash about at first and when they realised they were free, they bounded out of the water and into the bush. Some would stop and look back before they disappeared.

Then came a relay of men carrying sacks. They untied the openings and a variety of animals crawled out. First, a mongoose hesitantly sniffed at the air and skittered away. Next, appeared a sack that looked like it was about to explode! A feisty honey badger escaped and duly attacked the sack in its rage at being captured. A little later, a cage was offloaded, and a porcupine, rattling his quills, emerged toddling along like a mighty chief with a stately headdress.

Mai Guru spotted a man; she recognised by his long trousers and bucket hat. He too was carrying a sack. He walked further away to an outcrop of rocks. He bent down, untied the rope with care, and stepped back quickly. Out slithered an enormous black mamba.

Even a chameleon was saved and placed on a branch in a nearby bush. The local rangers would not touch it. They could not shake the traditional superstition that chameleons brought bad omens. After all, they are mysterious creatures with their ability to change colour, their eyes that swivel in all directions, and their rocking, hesitant style of walking.

The elephants watched as these animals ran free. They knew that what these men were doing was good, for without them all these creatures would not have survived.

25

Chapter Six

Crackers

▲▼

One evening, when the rangers had spent the day setting up the base camp, we decided to go to the new hotel at the top of the hill for dinner. In the middle of our meal, a man walked in and put a dog up on a table. There stood a little brown mongrel with some characteristics of a Dachshund and others of a Fox Terrier. The man proceeded to bang a glass to get everyone's attention. He announced, "I am leaving tomorrow. Does anyone want this dog?"

The little mutt had a cheeky look about him that Tinkey Haslam could not resist. Consequently, Crackers—as he was named—joined the rescue team and worked his way into the hearts of all the men.

Crackers took a particular liking to Rupert and followed him everywhere. Most days, he could be seen at the front of one of the boats with his ears flapping behind him on the lookout for animals in the water. When they landed on an island, he would disembark and join the team herding the animals towards the nets with his zealous barking. No animal scared him! He would take on zebra, or the antelopes—kudu, sable, or wildebeest. Crackers was fast and ducked and weaved any charge, persisting until the animal gave in. His assistance earned him respect and appreciation from the rangers.

Crackers' skills came to the fore when rescuing animals from aardvark burrow. Aardvarks are nocturnal animals rarely seen by people. Their skin is like a pig's. They have long noses and very powerful claws that they use to dig large tunnels, usually in an anthill, which they sleep in during the day. The men learned that aardvark claws were to be avoided as they are razor-sharp. Rex had his hand badly cut up when he held one aardvark by the ears. He did not know that its back legs can stretch right up to its head.

Crackers would disappear down the aardvark hole without hesitation. If he rapidly reversed out of the hole, barking furiously, the rangers knew there were one or more animals down the hole. Often there were several different tunnels, all interconnected. It would take some time to locate the aardvark. On one occasion, Rupert was sitting on a mound nearby when suddenly, the earth under him erupted and he was thrown into the air with soil flying everywhere. An aardvark emerged out of the dust.

On another occasion, the rangers were pursuing a porcupine when it disappeared down an aardvark hole. The aardvark did not like this prickly company and rushed out the other end, followed by a warthog and a baboon. Little antelope and wild cats were also found down these holes.

In the water, Crackers learned to use floating logs to run along as his little legs weren't the best at swimming. On the boat, his nimble feet would skip along the top of jerry cans and other equipment as he followed an animal in the water.

On the rare occasion when he had to stay behind, Crackers would sulk miserably, and choose to adopt another person to follow around. True to his gregarious nature, he added the orphan animals in camp to his collection of friends. He kept them entertained with many games of tag.

He added much fun to everyone's day.

A film clip of Crackers can be seen on YouTube Operation Noah, Part 3 at 10:05 minutes

27

But if from there you seek the LORD your God, you will find him if you seek him with all your heart and with all your soul.

Deuteronomy 4: 29

AARDVARK

Crackers

Chapter Seven

Base Camp and Orphan Animals

▲▼▲▼▲▼▲▼▲▼▲▼▲▼▲▼▲▼▲▼▲▼▲▼▲▼▲▼▲▼▲▼▲▼▲▼

Rex Bean and his wife, Gwen, took responsibility for the base camp, which was set up at Peter's Point, on the Rhodesian side, near the new dam wall. We were so appreciative of their practical care.

In the beginning, we used rope to tie the animals' legs but soon realised it rubbed the animals' limbs causing harm. A request was put out through The Society for the Prevention of Cruelty to Animals for ladies' stockings. An overseas newspaper featured a story titled, Wild Game Wearing Silk Stockings. A flood of bales from ladies in Britain, America, and South Africa descended on the camp. These stockings were braided together to make ropes.

There were times when we set up temporary camps on the islands. Rex would load up a boat and join us with food to feed the masses and the essential mosquito nets that we slept under. Our days were very long and physically demanding. One evening on returning, I was so exhausted that I fell asleep walking up the hill. Fellow rangers, Tinkey and Tommy came alongside, helping me make it to my bed.

The most critical victims of the flood were the young animals, including birds. Often during a rescue

Diary entry – 17th November 1958

The site selected on 17th November 1958, from which all operations are to be conducted by the game department in the future lake area, is situated on a barren rocky ridge overlooking the Zambezi and its confluence with the Sanyati river.

He brought me out into a wide and safe place. He saved me because he was pleased with me.

Psalm 18:19 (NIV)

BUSH BABY

30

operation, we would find a young animal alongside the dead body of its mother. We took these orphans back to camp to feed and care for until they were mature enough to be released into the wild. A baby baboon and a tiny vervet monkey, who had become friends, would sit for hours grooming each other. Rupert nicknamed them Zambezi and Sanyati. Sanyati seemed to think Zambezi was his mother and would often cling to her tummy as they walked around camp seeking out mischief.

Some of the cutest orphans were the bush babies with their big round eyes and their tiny hands. One particularly small one was rescued from the top of a tree. It was very weak. When the men got it back to camp, it was fed grapes and grasshoppers dipped in sugar to revive it. Then, we put it to bed in a shoe box.

In addition to these orphan babies, we cared for animals that had been injured. A warthog strained the muscles in his leg when resisting capture. He chose to make the outside toilet—also known as the

P.K. standing for Picaninni Kia - meaning little house—his home, much to the horror of a lady visitor.

Rupert insisted a python be allowed to live in the kitchen at night to prevent theft of the food. The tanks with the snakes were lined up on one side of the camp. One of the most impressive specimens was a two-metre-long cobra. I had a laboratory that the men insisted was downwind of the camp. This was because of the terrible smell of formaldehyde— which I used to preserve the specimens.

The largest of the animals in the camp was a rhino who was kept in a pen constructed of thick timber logs. One day, this poor animal developed a severe tummy ache. Its belly was bloated, and it began to roll on the ground squealing in pain. Rupert contacted the veterinarian who prescribed an enema which was a very complicated task on a rhino. This involved sticking a pipe up its rectum and pouring fluid in to force out the faeces!

BABY BABOON

VERVET MONKEY

31

Chapter Eight

Intriguing Observations

▼▲▼▲▼▲▼▲▼▲▼▲▼▲▼▲▼▲▼▲▼▲▼▲▼▲▼▲

I found it fascinating to spend time watching the animals, especially their efforts to save themselves and others. Kudu antelope swimming the long distance from an island to the mainland would regain their energy by sucking in air. This made them more buoyant. Leopards, waterbuck, bushbuck, and elephant, all proved to be the best long-distance swimmers. I was impressed by the very elegant swimming style of the genets. Genets are long cat-like animals with short legs and a tail that is as long as its body, which helps it balance. This swimming style was only matched by the chameleon with its long, controlled strokes. I learned that squirrels and bush babies are the poorest swimmers, only managing about ten metres.

One day, I was watching a waterbuck herd. I noticed that the doe supported her calf by allowing it to rest its head on her rump, like a flotation cushion. When the doe struggled, the ram then gave her support.

Bushbuck calves often got into difficulty. On one occasion, Rupert and two of the rangers swam alongside them, holding their heads up. Then, when the bushbuck could touch the bottom, the men put their arms under their bellies until they could walk free.

How many are your works, LORD!
In wisdom you made them all;
the earth is full of your creatures.
There is the sea, vast and spacious,
teeming with creatures beyond number—
living things both large and small

Deuteronomy 4: 29

Skin-divers

AS the floodwater rose day by day, the rescuers worked methodically, learning new tricks as they went. There was no time to do otherwise.

Frank Junor, one of the original "Three Musketeers" rescue party, discovered that monkeys are natural skin-divers.

Chasing one under water, he went down more than 15ft. The pressure on his lungs then forced him to surface. But the monkey was still going deeper.

Frank's theory was that monkeys turn submarine to protect themselves against crocodiles. He believes that the crocodile never seizes its prey when totally submerged. Only when it breaks surface will it pounce.

If true, this is a major scientific discovery.

It will take time to sift the findings of the men of Kariba. Their reports will be backed by some fascinating photographs.

Irish-born ex-wartime fighter pilot Terry Spencer spent weeks photographing the rescue operation. He took as many risks as any of the rangers.

Risks are his business. In the war he photographed the invasion coast ahead of D-Day. He was shot down, taken prisoner, and escaped.

Early one morning, we spotted a flash of white darting amongst the bushes. This caught our interest as it wasn't quite like anything we had seen before. We set out to capture this mysterious creature. It was a albino Sharpe's Grysbok, a rare little antelope!

The rangers made many first-time observations, writing them in their journals each evening after a long, hard day's work. Years later, this was very useful information for people studying African animals.

Sable extremely tired vs fresh, fast swimming

Mother Pangolin with her babe

Diary entry – 17th November 1958

Ranger Fothergill and I were surprised to see forty-odd vervet monkeys sitting in a Matombo tree on a submerged island. We observed that vervet monkeys are capable of diving under the water and remaining submerged for anything from 15 to 30 seconds, and that they continue to swim while underwater. I tried to follow one underwater as it descended to a depth of about 15 feet (4,57 metres).

33

Chapter Nine

Birds' Paradise

▲▽

While travelling between the islands we took notice of the weaver birds. No sooner had they built their nests when the waters rose and flooded them. The gritty little birds added another layer like a double-story house. The waters soon engulfed these nests too, but they kept at it building even higher. This resulted in them breeding out of season. They were very determined to make sure their species survived.

Jacanas are birds with huge feet. We nicknamed them lily trotters because they ran over the thick mat of salvinia weed so easily. They fed on the huge harvest of dead insects whose burrows had been flooded.

Bee-eaters flew in formation landing in their bolt holes burrowed in the riverbanks. Inquisitive hornbills tapped out their greeting on tree trunks. Malachite kingfishers flashed their brilliant colours, as they dived like jet pilots into the water to spear their prey. Migratory birds including flamingos stopped in to visit this new mass of water. The lake had become a birds' paradise.

We learned that land birds such as guinea fowl and franklin are poor fliers over a distance. They could swim but couldn't take off from the water, so the team would come alongside and scoop them up with nets.

When I was climbing the low branches to capture snakes, I noticed many chicks in nests that would be underwater before they were mature enough to fly. I suggested we create artificial nests, made of reeds, at the base camp for them. One man's sole job became catching fish each day to feed the chicks. The more common species were fledgling fish eagles, goliath herons, cormorants and egrets. It was a happy day when the saddle-billed storks tried their wings, flew around camp, and took off.

I had a particular fascination for fish-eating birds, and later when based at Kyle Dam, in south-east Rhodesia, I studied them for my master's degree.

Len and I were visiting an island one evening when we found two goliath heron chicks that were too young to fly. One of the chicks had been attacked by a starving monkey and had lost one eye. It was a sad sight, and we treated the injured one's wounds. We also tried to feed it, but it brought up the fish. We had little hope for it and let it go. Thankfully, it joined the other fledgling between two rocks. It put its head on the breast feathers of the fledgling, who then covered it with its wing and there they lay. The next morning, they had disappeared.

Cormorant

African Fish Eagle

Egret

Carmine bee-eater

Weaver

Malachite kingfisher

Crested Franklin

Saddle-billed Stork

Ground Hornbill

Goliath Heron

Flamingo

Guinea Fowl

Jacana (Lily Trotter)

35

Chapter Ten

Rhino Rescue

▲▼

It wasn't long before we realised that large animals, particularly rhinos, would be difficult to rescue. Rhinos are very poor swimmers and were doomed to drown or starve if we could not come up with a plan to help them. While sitting around the fire at base camp, we brainstormed how we could rescue these solid tanks. We knew that there were rhinos on areas of land that were becoming islands. The food available to them was becoming less and less, making the threat of starvation more real with each passing moment.

So it was that, in May 1959, we made our first attempt at forcing a rhino off an island onto another that was linked to the mainland. Len dropped Rupert and California off in the shallows after driving the boat through the submerged treetops.

California was a member of the Sena tribe. He was wise in bushcraft and had worked with Danny and Rupert for several years. He developed a deep friendship with the men through a common love and respect for all creatures.

These two men cautiously tracked the rhino, always ensuring a climbing tree was within easy reach. Eventually, they spotted movement and glimpses of grey hide, and Rupert decided to fire a shot into the air to frighten the animal. We hoped this would result in it taking the plunge into the shallow water and crossing over to the mainland.

At first, the rhino became angry, snorting and charging. No matter how much noise they made, the rhino chose rather to attack than retreat, resulting in the men shimmying up the nearest trees. They nicknamed it Greta Garbo, after a famous actress. Later, they discovered it was a male.

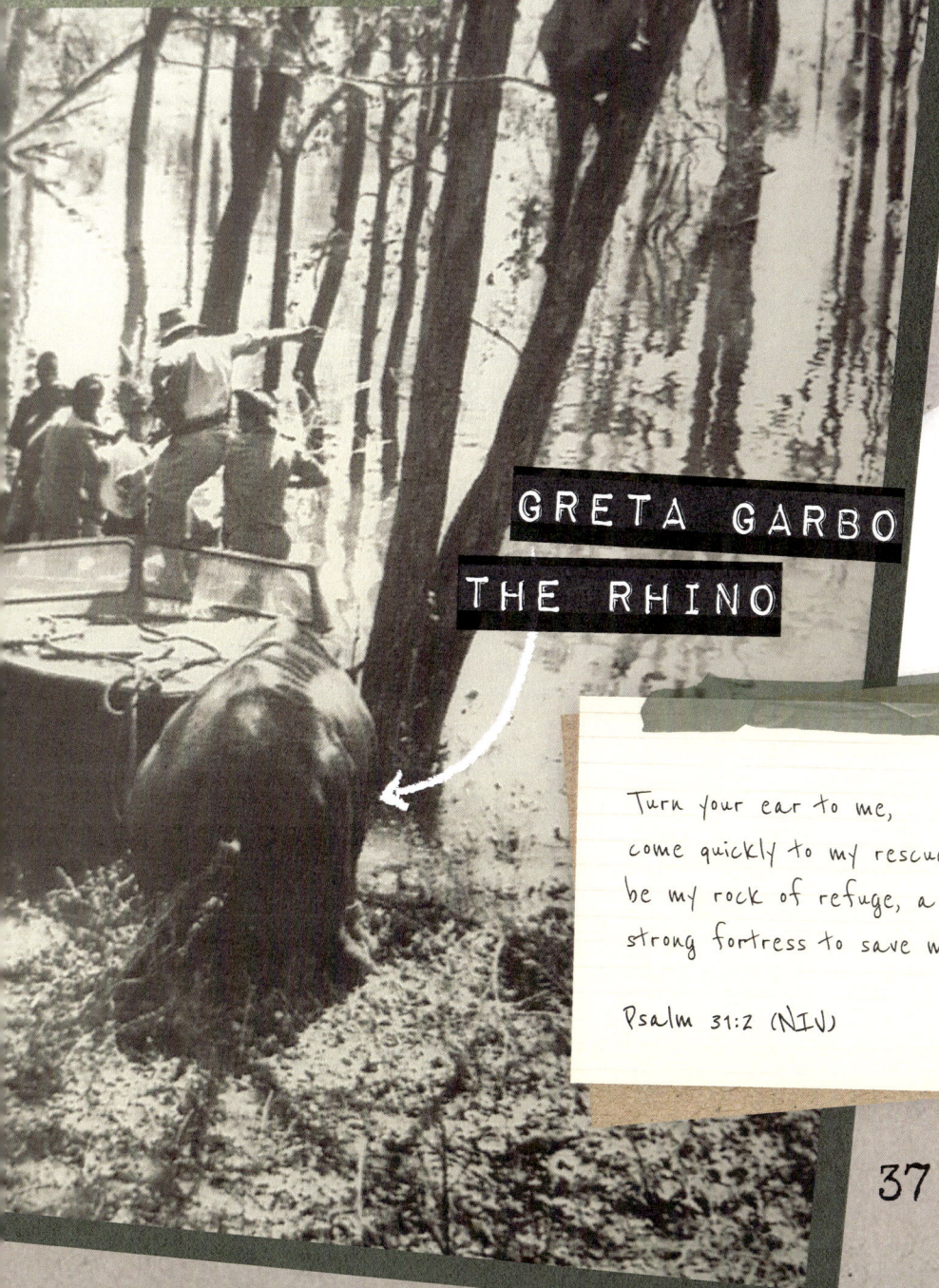

...k - get up the tree!

GRETA GARBO
THE RHINO

Turn your ear to me,
come quickly to my rescue;
be my rock of refuge, a
strong fortress to save me.

Psalm 31:2 (NIV)

37

All morning up and down the island they went, coming close but at the last minute, Greta chose to charge rather than enter the water.

In desperation, that afternoon with the heat getting them down, Rupert tried firing shots into the tree beside its head, without success. We even tried banging jerry cans creating a loud, annoying ruckus, but this only resulted in the rhino charging the boat. Thankfully, Len managed to turn the boat just in time. Unfortunately, after a difficult day without success, the operation to save this rhino was called off.

Later that evening, when a reporter questioned Rupert as to why he resorted to this method, he replied, "I couldn't very well tuck the rhino under one arm, St. Francis style, and carry him off."

Rescue of other animals continued, and it was only on the 2nd of July, that I went with Len back to the island. We were devastated to find Greta dead. On close examination, it looked like he had died of pneumonia, a lung infection brought on by poor eating and stubbornness. We became more determined than ever to find a way to rescue these magnificent beasts.

Chapter Eleven
Rhino Rescue - Take Two

From then on, we focused on finding a way to rescue rhinos. A pilot offered to swoop down low over the island, but this only resulted in the rhino trying to charge the plane. A veterinarian, John Condy, visited to investigate the possibility of using tranquilising darts.

In the meantime, we designed a raft and a sleigh. We were given the materials from the dam-building team: eighteen empty 44-gallon drums, planks, and wire. The sleigh was built in a V-shape to make it easier to drag. The rhino would be rolled onto the sleigh and dragged by thirty men to the water's edge where the rhino would be transferred onto a raft and towed by The Ark—one of the appropriately named larger boats.

On a clear, still morning the team set off to Rhino Island 2 with Dr Haarthoorn, a veterinarian. The rhino to be rescued was a large bull with an exceptionally bad temper. Having located the rhino in the dense bush, it proved to be very difficult to get a clear view. They tracked the rhino, listening for the crack of branches, or the snort of its heavy breathing. A few times, they were close enough to smell the distinct rhino odour but were never in a position to see the animal clearly enough to get in a shot. At lunchtime, we regrouped and devised another strategy. Dr Haarthoorn was to hide in the Jessie bush with a dart gun and the rest of the team were to make a huge noise driving the rhino past him.

Dr. Haarthoorn loaded the tranquilliser dart and held his breath in anticipation. The sound of the men beating cans came nearer. He would only have a few seconds to take the shot. Suddenly, the rhino appeared very agitated and moving fast. Just for a moment, it slowed to a trot, creating the perfect opportunity to fire. The dart landed in the underside of the leg where the skin was thinner, and the blood flow was good. He gave the thumbs up to the Rangers.

It would take some time for the tranquilliser to take effect. It was important to keep track of the rhino as it soon vanished from sight. They fanned out to locate it. Rupert spotted it and scaled a tree to avoid the now groggy rhino. It stood at the base of that tree shakily looking up with a penetrating glare. Rupert whistled to the team as it sank to the ground.

The rangers tied the rhino's legs together and rolled the sleepy animal onto the sleigh. The large team leaned in and hauled the sled to the waiting raft. This was the ultimate test; would it float and travel through the rough water? The mainland was twelve kilometres away.

Loading a rhino onto a sled

A Rhino is being towed on a raft

Rupert "greeting" the rhino

Rhino awakes

This capture can be seen in the following YouTube clips: Operation Noah | part 1, part 2, and part 3

39

The journey took ninety minutes and went without a hitch. On reaching the mainland, the sled was pulled ashore and the ropes on the rhino untethered. It didn't move … Rupert took a can of water and poured it over the rhino which woke with a start! The men ran for cover. The rhino charged the boat, tossing a can in the air and the boat with the crew beat a hasty retreat. The first rhino rescue was successful!

Forty-two more rhinos were rescued in this way. Chippy, the fifth rhino to be rescued, put her horn through the boat three times. She then focused her anger on Rupert, who was standing on the raft. He wasn't perturbed. He took off his hat and swatted the rhino several times on the head. Eventually Chippy gave up. When a journalist told Rupert he had captured the scene on camera, Rupert responded, "I was just waving farewell to Chippy."

The tenth rhino was a half-grown male on an island off the Bumi Hills. The drug did not work as well as it should, and the rhino became very aggressive; it kept charging the men. Once again, it chose to focus its attention on Rupert who was always close to the action. He ran as fast as he could and hid behind a fallen baobab tree, but much to his dismay, it had been eaten by ants. The rhino charged straight through the tree without any resistance pinning Rupert underneath it. There was an eruption of dust, stomping, and snorting making it very hard for the men to see Rupert. They did everything to distract the rhino. For a split second, the raging animal looked up and Rupert managed to wriggle out from between its back legs.

In true Rupert form, he only had a medical check a week later, and the doctors found that besides the cuts and bruises, he had six broken ribs!

A film crew used a plane to record one capture. As a prank, Rupert wrote 'Jean' in whitewash on the side of the rhino. He was teasing me as that was the name of my girlfriend who later became my wife. All of Rhodesia seemed to have watched this footage and I was teased quite a lot.

How to build a rhino raft:

1. Plan and prepare

- Select a flat, open area to assemble the raft.
- Lay out the oil drums in a line, evenly spaced apart.
- Measure and cut the wooden planks to fit across the oil drums, creating a platform. Ensure they overlap the drums slightly for stability.

2. Attach the wooden planks

- Place the planks across the oil drums, arranging them parallel to each other.
- Use wire to secure the planks to the drums tightly. Wrap the wire around the planks and the drums, twisting it securely. Ensure the planks are firmly attached to prevent movement.

3. Reinforce and secure

- Check the stability of the platform. Add additional planks if needed for reinforcement.
- Use screws or nails to further secure the planks to the oil drums. This will provide additional stability and prevent the planks from shifting.

4. Test the raft

- Before launching the raft into the water, check its stability and weight-bearing capacity on land or in shallow water.
- Ensure there are no loose parts and that the raft floats evenly without tilting excessively.

What you'll need:

- **Empty oil Drums:**
  Make sure they are sealed and have no holes. We needed 18 to carry the weight of a rhino.

- **Wooden Planks:**
  Sturdy enough to create a stable platform.

- **Wire or rope:**
  Strong and durable.

- **Tools:**
  Hammer, nails, saw, drill, screwdriver, measuring tape.

Chapter Twelve

Saving Snakes

▼▲

Many dangerous snakes lived in the Kariba Valley including the black mamba, the most venomous African snake. Although snakes are good swimmers, during this flood, they preferred to take refuge in the branches of trees that were slowly submerging. If a mamba decided to drop into a boat, from its shelter in the branches onto the occupants of the boat, they had only a split second to decide whether to try to kill the snake or jump overboard into the water where crocodiles often roamed.

I did not fear snakes, but I had great respect for them. My fascination with snakes started when I was a boy and continued into adulthood. My friends would warn others not to open the bottom drawer of my bedroom cupboard for fear of finding a little more than they might expect.

As a young man, my friend, Chips, and I would go out along the roads after it had rained to collect the frogs that had been squashed by the cars to feed to my pet snakes. One day, I was bitten by a burrowing adder, and I went to the hospital where they injected me with the anti-venom. A few days later, I broke out in a rash, had a very high temperature, and my joints went stiff. It turned out that I was allergic to the serum. This did not deter me one bit.

I taught myself the art of capturing a snake with a long rod that had a curve on the end like a shepherd's crook. I also kept a pair of thick leather gloves with my equipment.

So, it came to be that I got the job of capturing the snakes; not that I had much competition for the job. Often, while travelling through the branches in the boats or when walking through the bush, a call would be made for me: "Frank, nyoka [snake]". I would climb up after the snake wearing only my swimmers and gloves. I would slip the noose over the snake's head and draw it firm, holding the head furthest away from me. Then, I would drop it into a sack, held by one of the men. He would tie it firmly shut. I needed to be good at climbing and keeping my balance. At such times, I needed to have good focus and remain very calm. I believed it was easier to catch a snake in a tree because it did not move as quickly as it did on the ground.

We sent a wide variety of snakes to the snake park to ensure a specimen of each species was protected. The collection included Egyptian cobras, puff-adders, boomslangs, garter snakes, and pythons.

The LORD said to Moses, "Make a snake and put it up on a pole; anyone who is bitten can look at it and live.

Numbers 21: 8 (NIV)

Diary entry

I chased a large hissing sand snake out of a tree into the water. Rex was very concerned because he was convinced that it was a mamba. I caught it while it was swimming, and it bit my gloved left thumb; it held on like a bulldog. It was therefore placed in a bag, glove and all.

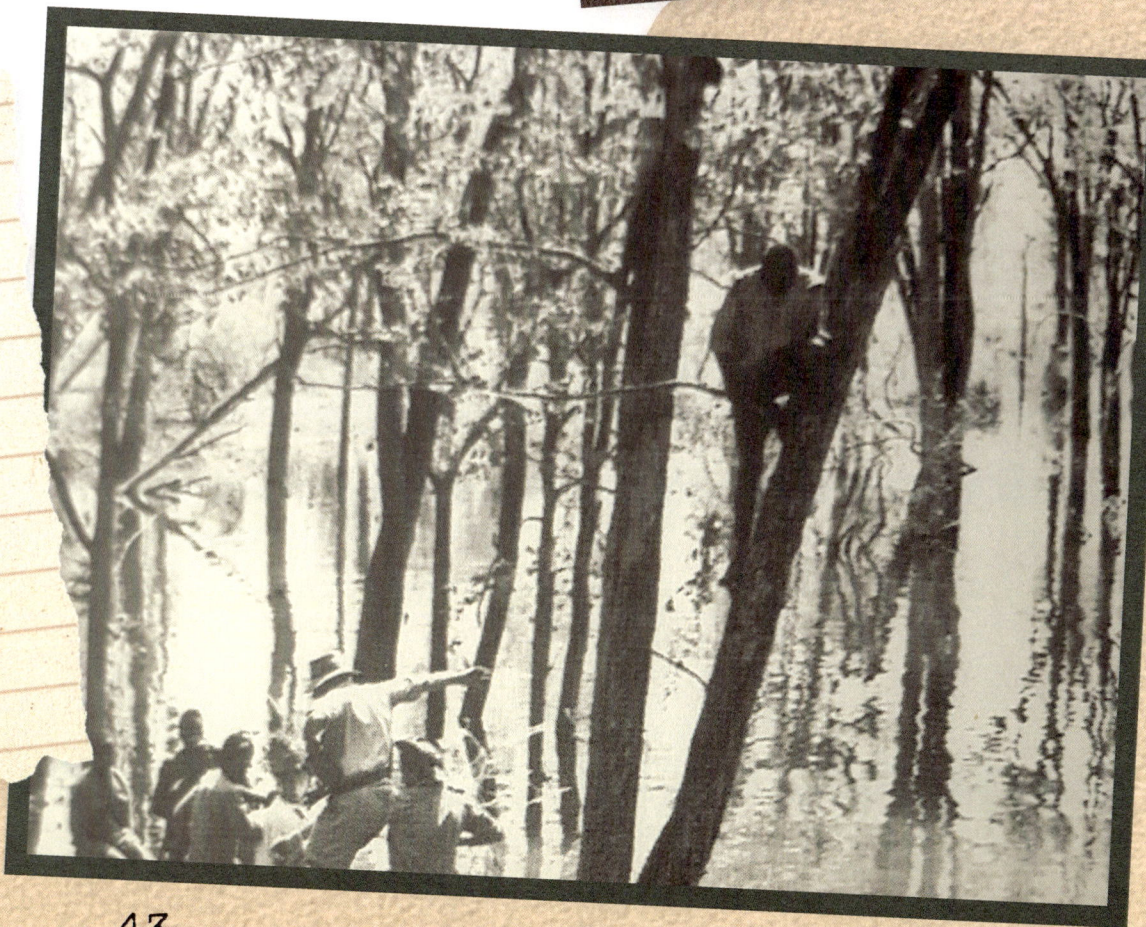

Chapter Thirteen

Buffalo Encounter

Every day, our men encountered dangers of many kinds and risked being wounded. On the 4th of March, California and I climbed off the boat to search on an island that was rapidly submerging.

At the same moment that we spotted the fresh tracks of a buffalo, the huge mammal came charging out of the bushes toward us! I quickly jumped behind a mopani tree. The buffalo swung its horns wildly trying to attack but it became distracted by California running in the other direction. I caught a branch and swung up into a tree. I watched anxiously as I saw California running into the water just ahead of the enraged bull. Luckily, the mud at the water's edge slowed it down. California dived down into the water, realising that it was not deep enough to protect him. He rapidly buried himself in the mud.

After splashing around in the shallows, the buffalo eventually lost interest and left. From my place in the tree, I saw California emerge from the water coated in mud. We returned to the boat a little shaken by the close encounter.

On the 7th of March, Len, Barry, and I went ashore on the same island. It had been divided up into smaller pieces by the rising water. There were no buffalo to be seen but many signs they had been there recently. Finding nothing we decided to go back to the boat. Barry and Len got side-tracked following some waterbuck spoor.

As I walked along, the hairs on the back of my neck stood up. I had a strange feeling that something was watching me. A bone-chilling snort shattered the silence! Charging through the brush was the same buffalo bull. This time, there was no tree. I turned to run but the buffalo caught me. It pierced my leg with its horn and tossed me into the air. I fell on top of its head which winded me me. Then, I was tossed up again. This time, I fell in front of the buffalo's legs. Somehow, I found the breath to call for help. I could smell the beast's hot breath and saw the crazed look in its eye. It kept trying to crush me. I dug deep and mustered my strength to push its head just far enough away. I was fast losing strength as a searing pain kept shooting through my leg.

Barry and Len heard my cry and rushed to my rescue. At first, Barry could not take a shot because I was underneath the crazed mammal. Barry ran round to the side and shot into its stomach. Then, Len let off another shot. The Buffalo took off, and only after the sixth shot, did it drop.

I was bleeding heavily from the hole in my left leg. Barry took off his shirt and stuffed it in the wound to slow the blood flow. They wrapped up the injury the best they could and carried me to the boat. I was taken to Kariba Hospital where they

This is how we know what love is: Jesus Christ laid down his life for us. And we ought to lay down our lives for our brothers and sisters.

1 John 3:16 (NIV)

The buffalo

BUFFALO PUT HIM IN HERE

Frank Junor, in a Kariba hospital bed after his encounter with a buffalo, is cheered up by Len Harvey, right, and Barry Ball, who shot the buffalo, left. On the extreme left is Brian Hughes, another ranger in the small hard-worked party.

KARIBA RESCUE RANGER IS GORED BY A BUFFALO

Evening Standard Correspondent
Kariba, Wednesday.

THE first major casualty in the game rescue operations on Lake Kariba, Game Ranger Frank Junor, is now recovering in Kariba hospital, after being gored by a buffalo.

Frank Junor, with two other rangers, Barry Ball and Len Harvey, had started slowly to beat an island, some 40 or more miles up the lake from the dam site.

It was not thought that there was anything big left on the island, but as game sometimes returns, after being driven from land to swim to the next island, a check was being made.

Frank became separated from the other two members of the party, and hearing a sound, he turned just in time to see a full grown buffalo making for him from about 20 feet away.

He had no time to do anything before he was caught and one of his legs badly gored.

FIRST TIME

The other two men came to his assistance, and Barry Ball, who was carrying a rifle for the first time during these game recovery operations, killed the buffalo from 30 yards before it had a chance to gore Mr. Junor again.

Another few seconds' delay on the part of his companions, and the tale might have had a tragic ending.

But ... ree rangers ...

light of the matter, and standing round the bed in the hospital ward they chatted about latest progress, and new islands visited.

In response to a question of how they thought volunteer helpers would get on, said that they thought it would be more trouble than help.

WOULD GET LOST

With the vast areas the lake now covers, inexperienced helpers would get completely lost.

The dangers, although they would be the first to deny it, are very real.

After seeing the small team return from almost a week away from base camp, covered with scratches and festering wounds that have little chance to heal, it is clear that the risks are not only from wild animals.

The team now operating consists of five men, one injured, one on compassionate leave, and three still toiling.

---

repaired the tendons, muscles, and skin in the back of my leg. I was given an anti-tetanus injection despite my objecting strongly. Sure enough, ten days later, my eyes swelled shut, a lump came up on my head, and I suffered severe chest pains with my pulse racing violently. I was allergic to the anti-tetanus serum.

Len and Barry worked out that the buffalo must have hidden in the shallow water behind some submerged trees. It had waited in ambush for us. They noted that it had a stiff leg from a previous injury. This explained why it was so aggressive but could not crush me. Many times, when animals attack people, it is because they have previously been wounded.

Many men were wounded by frightened animals when attempting to rescue them. It was only as a last resort, when someone's life was in danger, that we had to shoot the attacking animal. A scout, Sarachekepa, had a piece taken out of his finger and was knocked flat by a bushpig; Len had his elbow smashed by a little duiker's rapid kick; and Rupert was gored by a rhino. Despite these wounds, all of us believed it was worth it.

All in all, over 6000 animals were saved.

POST OFFICE TELEGRAPHS.—POSKANTOORTELEGRAAFDIENS.

URGENT. DRINGEND.

CAUSEWAY RHOD 87 9TH 0950=

ZG67 CZA94 YCA61 CSY700 ETATBG

URGENT= A JUNOR ESQ 12

LANSDOWNROAD GRAHAMSTOWN=

403 TO FORESTALL ANY UNDUE WORRY WHICH MAY BE CAUSED

TO YOU BY EXAGGERATED NEWSPAPER ATEE REPORTS

I WISH TO ADVISE THAT YOUR SON FRANK HAD UNFORTUNATE

ENCOUNTER WITH BUFFALO WHEN ENGAGED IN GAME CONTROL

OPERATION AT KARIBA ON SUNDAY 8TH MARCH STOP FRANK

POST OFFICE TELEGRAPHS.—POSKANTOORTELEGRAAFDIENS.

RECEIVING FROM INJURIES TO HIS LEGS AND SHOCK

ATKARIBA HOSPITAL STOP SURGEON AND DOCTOR IN ATTENDANCE

STOP KARIBA HOSPITAL REPORT FRANK COMFORTABLE AND

CHEERFUL THIS MORNING STOP FRANK WRITING TO YOU TODAY =

GAME OFFICE SALISBURY+ !

FIS 12 403 8TH

47

Epilogue
The Marula Tree

Shingi is no longer the little one. Shingi is now the matriarch of the elephant herd. They travel part of the ancient path and have created a new route below the mighty concrete fortress of Kariba Dam. They must be careful, for they have new threats. There are men with guns that have many bullets: they are poachers who want their ivory tusks to sell.

One morning, some of these men lay in wait for the herd. As they walked down into a small valley a sharp sound shattered the silence. Mayhem erupted! Flying pieces of timber, leaves, and dust exploded over them as the herd stampeded, taking off with shrieking, trumpeting cries.

The charging elephants only stopped when they reached the plain. They huddled together trembling in fear and aftershock. It was then that Shingi realised that her mother was not with them. She had been leading the herd and had been pierced by most of the bullets. At the loss of their leader and friend, the sad giants grieved together, mulling around, and comforting each other with deep, sorrowful rumblings, touching each other with their trunks. They could not go forward without returning to the scene of the trauma. So, a few days later, they gathered courage and returned. There they found her body: her beautiful ivory tusks had been hacked out of her head.

It was now time for Shingi to take over the role of lead matriarch of the herd.

On their adapted route, they now travel through the deep Zambezi River gorge spending time in the thick bush where they are well hidden. At the time of the year when the marula fruit are ripening, they climb the steep mountain, out of the valley. Elephants have an excellent sense of smell and when upwind, they can pick up minute particles of an odour floating in the air. The young ones get excited from far off as they smell the fruit of their favourite marula tree. It always bears fruit earlier than the other trees. It is in the garden of the man who was on the boat that fateful day when they couldn't find their way. They have been to this garden before. Shingi will never forget his voice, his long trousers, and his bucket hat.

48

When they stop to feast, that same man stands on his veranda, with his four daughters. He has been known to throw oranges to add to the feast. There is a silent connection between the man and the elephant matriarch. Shingi knows that the herd is safe with him. Sadly, she doesn't know how to keep her herd from the danger of greedy men who are not like this kind man.

Shingi wonders: In years to come, will the man's grandchildren and great-grandchildren get to meet hers?

Acknowledgements

Rhodesian/ Zimbabwean children going to school in the 60s and 70s had, as part of their weekly routine, educational movies. Frequently, one of those movies would be Operation Noah. The story became a national legend, one that docs not include politics. It tells of a team of men, both black and white, who united in a cause: they had a driving passion to save animals along the Zambezi River whilst Kariba Dam was being built on the border between Zambia and Rhodesia from 1958 to 1964

Change to: It tells of a team of men, both black and white, who united over a common passion to save wildlife. The mission was to rescue as many animals as possible from drowning whilst Kariba Dam was being built from 1958 to 1964. With very limited resources or precedent, they committed to rescuing animals from the rising waters of the Zambezi River as it backed up behind the newly constructed dam wall at Kariba. In all, the men rescued over 6,000 animals.

When I visit the homes of Zimbabweans (formerly Rhodesians) scattered throughout the world, the pictures on their walls and the decoration of their homes reflect the love of wildlife and the natural beauty of Zimbabwe. It is central to Zimbabwean culture.

I chose to write this story for my grandchildren, as I want them to know about my country of origin. I want them to learn about the heritage that has been passed on to them from their great-grandfather, Frank Junor, who led the research in Operation Noah.

This story is also for all children, as it is an important example of mankind taking responsibility for the care of our wildlife and our planet. Creation and mankind are bound together; they are directly affected by each other's actions.

My primary resources have been my father's diary and 16mm film. My sister, Colleen, organised for him to commentate while recording the story onto video. Like many people, as we get older, and often when it is too late, we become aware that we should have had many more conversations with our parents about their life experiences: I am no exception. Hence, I am very grateful for the resources in the following:

- Animal Dunkirk by Eric Robins and Ronald Legge
- Rupert Fothergill: Bridging a Conservation Era by Keith Meadows
- Operation Noah by Charles Lagus
- Operation Noah video footage on YouTube that was compiled by Ron Thomson and provided by the Fothergill family.

I am grateful to my sister Diana Walker for taking care of my dad's resources and my sister Helen Dutoit for the beautiful sketch of the elephants with their heads together. And last but not least, to my niece Carmen Ladwig who created the phenomenal graphic designs, thank you.

www.ingramcontent.com/pod-product-compliance
Lightning Source LLC
Chambersburg PA
CBRC090216310326
41914CB00096B/1653